Handbook for Reading

Phonics Textbook

Fourth Edition

abeka.

Pensacola, FL 32523-9100
an affiliate of PENSACOLA CHRISTIAN COLLEGE®

Note to Parents and Teachers

Handbook for Reading may be used at any level for initial teaching of phonics and reading, for reinforcement of skills, or for remedial work. By mastering the simple phonics sounds in this book, any person will be well on his way to becoming a skillful reader. It may be used with an entire class, with small groups, or with individuals at home.

A Teacher Edition and other helpful aids—*Basic Phonics Sounds CD, Basic Phonics Charts,* and *Basic Phonics Flashcards*—are also available from Abeka.

The idea for *Handbook for Reading* came from Noah Webster's famous *American Spelling Book,* familiarly called *The Blue-Backed Speller,* which was first published in 1783. Webster's purpose in his book was two-fold: to teach reading and spelling by the phonics method, and to give wholesome, character-building reading material to America's youth. Abeka returns these important ideals to America's classrooms by the publication of phonics materials and Christian textbooks.

Handbook for Reading
Fourth Edition

Staff Credits
Authors: Margaret McCary, Laurel Hicks, Naomi Sleeth
Managing Editor: Corinne Sawtelle
Edition Editor: Tanya Harrington
Designer: Michelle Johnson
Production Artists: Susan Schmuck, Tammy McLaughlin
Cover Illustration: April Richards
Illustrators: Brian Jekel, Nadine Voth, Lauren Wilson, Peter Kothe, and Abeka staff

Acknowledgments
"Eletelephony" from *Tirra Lirra: Rhymes Old and New* by Laura E. Richards. Copyright 1930, 1932 by Laura E. Richards. Copyright © renewed 1960 by Hamilton Richards. By permission of Little, Brown and Company. All rights reserved.

Abeka, a Christian textbook ministry affiliated with Pensacola Christian College, is designed to meet the need for Christian textbooks and teaching aids. The purpose of this publishing ministry is to help Christian schools reach children and young people for the Lord and train them in the Christian way of life.

Cataloging Data
McCary, Margaret.
    Handbook for reading : phonics
    textbook / Margaret McCary, Laurel Hicks,
    Naomi Sleeth. – 4th ed.
    155 p. : col. ill. ; 22 cm.
    1. Reading – Phonetic method. II. Hicks, Laurel.
III. Sleeth, Naomi. IV. Abeka Book, Inc.
Library of Congress: PE1119 .H32 2015
   Dewey System: 418

Reading Program

Handbook for Reading (grades 1–3)
Primary Bible Reader (grades 1, 2)

1st
Fun with Pets
Tiptoes
Stepping Stones
Secrets and Surprises
Kind and Brave
Aesop's Fables
Strong and True
Down by the Sea
Animals in the
    Great Outdoors

2nd
Fun with Friends
Quests for Adventure
Across the Meadow
Wonders of Imagination
Through the Skies
Growing Up in Early America
Growing Up around the World
Growing Up Where Jesus Lived
All Kinds of Animals
My New Name (novel)
Reading Comprehension 2
    Skill Sheets

3rd
From Shore to Shore
My New Song (novel)
Through the Seasons
Among the Animals
Pilgrim Boy (novel)
Treats and Treasures
Heroes and Helpers
Secret in the Maple Tree (novel)
On the Bright Side
The Swiss Family Robinson (novel)
Pilgrim's Progress:
    Christian's Journey (novel)
Reading Comprehension 3
    Skill Sheets

4th
Song of the Brook (novel)
Saved at Sea (novel)
Salute to Courage
Liberty Tree
Flags Unfurled
Trails to Explore
Read & Think 4 Skill Sheets
Adventures in Other Lands
    (Speed / Comprehension)

5th
Rosa (novel)
Noah Webster: A Man Who
    Loved Words (biography)
Beyond the Horizon
Windows to the World
Of America I
Read & Comprehend 5
    Skill Sheets
Adventures in Nature
    (Speed / Comprehension)

6th
Billy Sunday (biography)
Message of the Mountain (novel)
Mountain Pathways
Voyage of Discovery
Of America II
Reading Comprehension 6
    Skill Sheets
Adventures in Greatness
    (Speed / Comprehension)

7th –12th
Of People
Of Places
Themes in Literature
World Literature
American Literature
English Literature

abeka.

Contents

Six Easy Steps to Reading

1 Learn to recognize the short vowels and their sounds. (Chart 1)

2 Learn to recognize the consonants and their sounds. (Chart 2)

3 Learn to blend a consonant and vowel together. (Charts 3, 3A, 4)

4 Learn to sound one-vowel words. (Chart 4A)

5 Learn the sounds of the long vowels. (Chart 5) **Learn to sound two-vowel words.** (Chart 5A)

6 Learn and apply the special phonics sounds.

Additional Skills Learned in This Book

- Identify prefixes and suffixes.
- Recognize rhyming words, opposites, same meaning words, same sounding words, compound words, contractions, and related words.

The Short Vowels

Practice these sounds each day until you know them well.

Aa *Aa*

apple

Ee *Ee*

elephant

Ii *Ii*

inchworm

Oo *Oo*

ostrich

Uu *Uu*

umbrella

o   a   u   i   e

Chart 1

Aa   apple

Aa   *apple*

Listen to someone read these words. Do you hear the ă-apple sound?

1.   hat   cat   map

2.   jam   pan   man

Listen to someone read these pairs of words.
Repeat the word that has the ă-apple sound.

did – dad   as – is

cab – cub   lip – lap

Ee

Ee (cursive)

elephant

elephant (cursive)

Listen to someone read these words. Do you hear the ĕ-elephant sound?

1. **net** **fell** **pet**

2. **ten** **bed** **hen**

Listen to someone read these words.
Repeat the word that has the ĕ-elephant sound.

less – loss   not – net

tan – ten   get – got

Chart 1   3

Ii  inchworm

Ii *inchworm*

Listen to someone read these words. Do you hear the ĭ-inchworm sound?

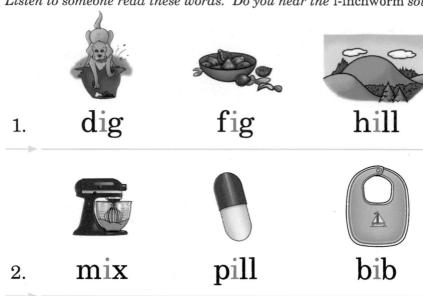

1.   dig   fig   hill

2.   mix   pill   bib

Listen to someone read these pairs of words.
Repeat the word that has the ĭ-inchworm sound.

hit – hot   mutt – mitt

zap – zip   lid – lad

Oo   ostrich

Oo   *ostrich*

Listen to someone read these words. Do you hear the ŏ-ostrich sound?

1. dog   top   doll

2. Tom   stop   pop

Listen to someone read these pairs of words.
Repeat the word that has the ŏ-ostrich sound.

top – tap   Ned – nod

Rick – rock   hot – hat

Chart 1   5

Uu

umbrella

𝒰 𝓊   umbrella

Listen to someone read these words. Do you hear the ŭ-umbrella sound?

1.   **bug**   **sun**   **bus**

2.   **tub**   **bun**   **gum**

Listen to someone read these pairs of words.
Repeat the word that has the ŭ-umbrella sound.

mud – mad   bin – bun

fan – fun   dug – dig

The Consonants

Practice these sounds each day until you know them well.

Ll	Tt	Bb
Mm	Rr	Ff
Dd	Gg	Ss
Cc	Nn	Hh
Yy	Jj	Ww
Kk	Xx	Qq
Zz	Pp	Vv

Chart 2   7

Ll  lamp

Ll *lamp*

Say the sounds.

a   e   i   o   u

Note: Blending the sounds of a consonant and a vowel is an important step to reading words. We always read from left to right.

Read the blends.

l → a → la

l → e → le

l → i → li

l → o → lo

l → u → lu

Read up and down the blend ladder.

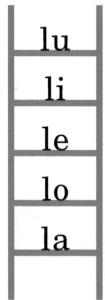

lu

li

le

lo

la

Tt

table

$\mathcal{T}t$

table

Say the sounds.

a	i	o	u	e

Read the blends.

Read up and down the blend ladder.

t → a ——→ ta

t → e ——→ te

t → i ——→ ti

t → o ——→ to

t → u ——→ tu

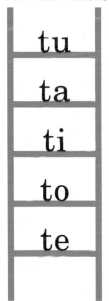

tu

ta

ti

to

te

Review

Say the sounds.

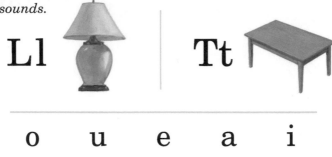

Ll   Tt

| o | u | e | a | i |

Note: When there is one vowel in a word, it usually says its short sound.

l → e — le → t — let

l → o — lo → t — lot

l → i — li → t — lit

t → o — to → t — tot

Read the words.

| let | lit | tell* |
| lot | tot | till* |

*The doubled consonant is pronounced only one time.

Bb

bell

B b

bell

Say the sounds.

l u o b t i

Say the blends.

ba
be
bi
bo
bu

Read the blends and then make words.

ba → t → bat

bi → t → bit

bu → t → but

tu → b → tub

Bo → b → Bob

Read the words.

bit   lot   tot   bat

tub   Bob   let   but

Review

l　　t　　b

Read across and then down.

	⚪	⬛	🔺	❤️
1.	a	la	ta	ba
2.	e	le	te	be
3.	i	li	ti	bi
4.	o	lo	to	bo
5.	u	lu	tu	bu
6.	bat	Bob	lot	tot
7.	lab	tab	bit	lit
8.	tell	till	bell	Bill

Read the sentence.

Tab bit Bob.

Tab bit Bob.

12　Charts 2–4A

Review

Read across and then down.

⚪	⬛	🔺	❤️
1. ta	lo	ti	bu
2. le	ba	lu	to
3. bi	tu	bo	le
4. to	le	ta	bi
5. tub	bit	let	tab
6. bat	tot	bill	lot

Read the sentence.

Let Bob tell Bill.

Let Bob tell Bill.

Mm

milk

Mm　　　　　　　　　*milk*

Ll 　　　Tt 　　　Bb

Say the short-vowel sounds. Read the blends. Read the words.
Read across and then down.

●	■	▲	♥	★
1.	a	e	i	o	u
2.	ma	me	mi	mo	mu
3.	mat	met	mill	Mom	mutt

Read the sight word and phrases.

Sight word:　*a (ŭ)

a bell	a mat
a tub	a bat

*Note: The word *a*, when used in a sentence, is usually
　　pronounced "ŭ."

Review

Say the sounds.

a	m	e	l	b
o	t	u	i	

Read across and then down.

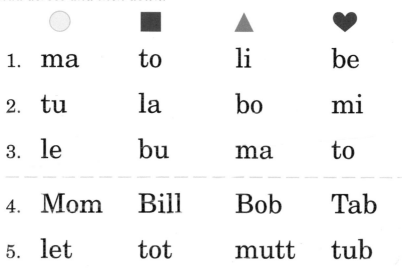

	○	■	▲	♥
1.	ma	to	li	be
2.	tu	la	bo	mi
3.	le	bu	ma	to
4.	Mom	Bill	Bob	Tab
5.	let	tot	mutt	tub

Read the sight word and sentence.

Sight word: *the (thŭ)

Tib met Tab at the mill.

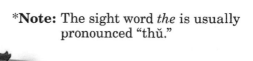

***Note:** The sight word *the* is usually pronounced "thŭ."

Rr   ring

Rr   *ring*

Read across and then down.

●	■	▲	♥	★
1. u	a	o	i	e
2. ru	ra	ro	ri	re
3. rub	rat	rob	rib	😊
4. ta	li	mu	be	lo
5. mi	lu	to	bi	la
6. mat	Mel	Bob	tab	mill
7. rat	bell	rob	Bab	Bill
8. bat	tell	mob	Rab	till

Ff

fox

Ff *fox*

Read across and then down. How fast can you read?

	●	■	▲	♥	★
1.	a	e	i	o	u
2.	fa	fe	fi	fo	fu
3.	fat	fell	fill	☺	☺
4.	re	mu	to	ba	li
5.	to	bi	ra	me	lu
6.	rat	fat	mat	tab	lab
7.	Mom	lot	tot	Bob	rot
8.	rib	lit	bit	fit	mill

Review

Say the sounds.

m	r	f	l	t	b

Read across and then down.

○	■	▲	♥
1. a	ma	ra	fa
2. e	me	re	fe
3. i	mi	ri	fi
4. o	mo	ro	fo
5. u	mu	ru	fu
6. mat	met	rub	tell
7. rat	let	tub	fell
8. fat	lit	lab	lot

A fat rat bit Tab.

Dd dog

Dd *dog*

	⬤	◼	▲	♥	★
1.	u	e	o	a	i
2.	du	de	do	da	di
3.	dull	dell	doll	Dad	dill
4.	ba	re	fi	lo	mu
5.	ti	fu	ra	me	bo
6.	let	met	fell	bell	tell

Read the sight words and phrases.

Sight words: the (thŭ), a (ŭ)

the red bib   a big bell

Gg   goat

Gg   *goat*

○	■	▲	♥	★
1. a	i	o	e	u
2. ga	gi	go	ge	gu
3. gal	gill	got	get	gum
4. ro	fu	ma	de	ti
5. dig	get	bag	dog	gull
6. Dad	God	Ted	Bill	Tom

Read the sight word and sentences.

Sight word: the (thŭ)

The big dog dug.
Bad dog!

Ss sun

𝓢𝓼 𝓼𝓊𝓃

Are you reading faster now?

●	■	▲	♥	★
1. i	u	o	a	e
2. si	su	so	sa	se
3. sit	sum	sod	sat	set
4. li	ta	bu	re	mo
5. fe	do	ga	la	bi
6. bag	beg	big	bog	bug
7. sat	fat	mat	bat	rat
8. led	fed	bed	Ted	red

Review

m	r	d	l	g	b	s	t

	○		■		▲		♥
1.	a		da		ga		sa
2.	e		de		ge		se
3.	i		di		gi		si
4.	o		do		go		so
5.	u		du		gu		su
6.	dug		dill		tell		God
7.	rug		sat		fell		sin
8.	mug		get		sell		fill

rab|bit

Cc

cat

Cc   *cat*

Say the sounds.

e	u	o	a	i

Read the blends. Add the final consonant. Read the words.

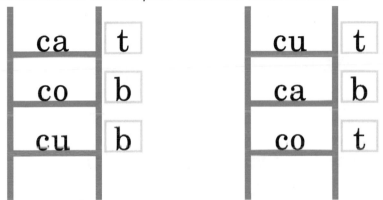

ca	t
co	b
cu	b

cu	t
ca	b
co	t

Read the sight words and phrases.

Sight words: the (thŭ), a (ŭ)

the cup   a cut

a big cat   the cab

a big cat   *the cab*

Nn

nest

Nn   *nest*

	●	■	▲	♥	★
1.	a	u	e	o	i
2.	na	nu	ne	no	ni
3.	Nan	nut	net	nod	nill
4.	Nan	tan	man	ran	Dan
5.	sod	rod	nod	God	Todd
6.	nut	but	cut	rut	jut

Read the sight words and sentences.

Sight words: a (ŭ), the (thŭ)

Ned has a bug.
The bug is in the rug.

Hh

horse

Hh

horse

How fast are you reading now?

●	■	▲	♥	★
1. a	o	u	e	i
2. ha	ho	hu	he	hi
3. hat	hot	hum	hen	hit
4. lid	did	hid	bid	Sid
5. gas	sad	bat	had	dab
6. met	get	set	let	net

Read the sight word and sentences.

Sight word: a (ŭ)

Mom fed Bill.

Bill had a hot dog.

Review

c	n	h	d	m	s	r	f

	○	■	▲	♥
1.	a	na	ha	hat
2.	e	ne	he	hen
3.	i	ni	hi	hill
4.	o	no	ho	hot
5.	u	nu	hu	hug
6.	can	cut	cap	cot
7.	nut	nap	not	nod
8.	ham	hop	hit	hum

mit|ten

hap|pen

Yy

Yy

yarn

yarn

●	■	▲	♥	★
1. e	a	i	u	o
2. yu	yi	ya	yo	ye
3. yam	yes	yet	yell	yum
4. ham	less	get	fell	gum
5. ram	mess	net	sell	sum

Sight word: a

Sam had a hat.

Sam had a big hat.

Sam had a big, red hat.

Jj jar

Jj *jar*

○	■	▲	♥	★
1. o	u	e	a	i
2. jo	ju	je	ja	ji
3. jog	jug	jell	jam	Jill
4. fell	dug	jet	hill	jam
5. bell	hug	net	Bill	ham

Hit it, Jim.
Jim hit it.
Jim had fun!

Ww  wagon

Ww *wagon*

	■	▲	♥	★
1. a	i	e	u	o
2. we	wa	wu	wo	wi

3. wag	rag	sag	tag	bag
4. bell	fell	well	jell	tell
5. nut	but	mutt	hut	rut
6. hop	top	pop	mop	stop

Tag is wet.
His rug is wet.

Review

y	j	n	w	t	m	s

	○	■	▲	♥
1.	a	ya	ja	wa
2.	e	ye	je	we
3.	i	yi	ji	wi
4.	o	yo	jo	wo
5.	u	yu	ju	wu
6.	yes	jog	wag	sag
7.	yell	jet	wet	gas
8.	yum	Jill	will	fun
9.	yip	job	well	fin

rib|bit

Kk  kite

𝒦𝓀 𝓀𝒾𝓉𝑒

Note: *K* comes before *i* and *e; c* comes before *a, o,* and *u.*

○	■	▲	♥	★
1. a	e	i	o	u
2. ca	ke	ki	co	cu
3. cat	Ken	kit	cob	cub
4. him	set	big	gum	bed
5. Kim	met	fig	hum	fed
6. Jim	let	dig	sum	led

Sight words: a, to, the

Jon sat on a log.

Jill went to the van.

Xx   fox box ax

Xx "ks"   *fox box ax*

Note: The *x* sound ("ks") comes at the end of a word, not at the beginning.

●	■	▲	♥	★
1. wax	tax	Max	lax	vex
2. box	fox	fix	mix	six
3. not	dot	hot	lot	cot
4. tub	hub	rub	cub	nub
5. mill	dill	sill	will	till

Jack has six cats.
Jill has six dogs.

Qu  queen

Qu *queen*

Note: *Q* and *u* are almost always together in a word.

⬤ ■ ▲ ♥

1.   a   e   i   o

2. qua   que   qui   quo

3. quick   quack   quit   quill

4. quit   sit   hit   fit

5. beg   peg   Meg   leg

Jan can run fast.
Will Jan quit?
No, Jan will not quit.

Review

ca	ke	ki	co	cu
qua	que	qui	quo	

Note: When there is one vowel in a word, it usually says its short sound. We mark it with a smile.

●	■	▲	♥	★
1. băd	dŭg	wĭn	jĕt	cŏt
2. hill	sell	gas	top	yell
3. Ken	Jim	mug	wag	fog
4. fan	bug	kiss	ham	den
5. not	get	ten	fun	Sam

kit|ten

Zz zebra

Zz *zebra*

○	■	▲	♥	★
1. i	u	a	o	e
2. zi	ze	zu	zo	za
3. fi	do	gu	se	ba
4. ma	ru	be	to	li
5. zig	zag	zip	bag	rug
6. bat	rat	mat	rut	sit

Sight word: the

in the bag   the big rug

in the bag   *the big rug*

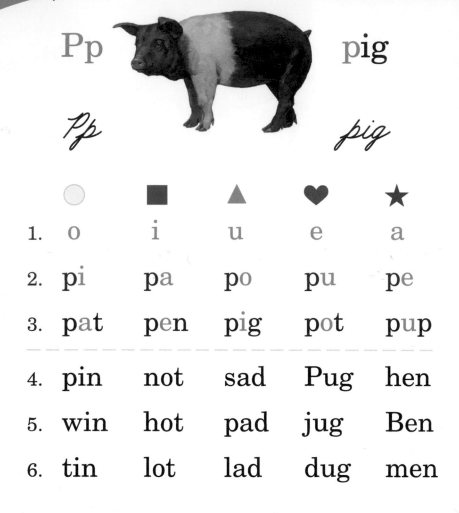

Pp   pig

Pp   *pig*

●	■	▲	♥	★
1. o	i	u	e	a
2. pi	pa	po	pu	pe
3. pat	pen	pig	pot	pup
4. pin	not	sad	Pug	hen
5. win	hot	pad	jug	Ben
6. tin	lot	lad	dug	men

Sight words: a, to

Pat has a dog.

Pat will run to his dog.

Vv 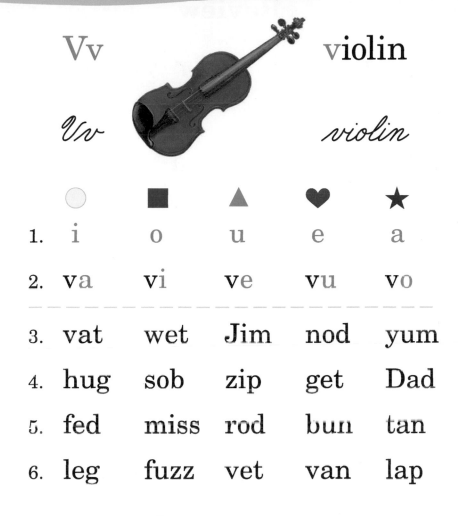 violin

Vv *violin*

●	■	▲	♥	★
1. i	o	u	e	a
2. va	vi	ve	vu	vo

3. vat   wet   Jim   nod   yum

4. hug   sob   zip   get   Dad

5. fed   miss   rod   bun   tan

6. leg   fuzz   vet   van   lap

Sight words: a, the

Dad has a van.
The van is red.

Review

d z p l v r k t g

◯	■	▲	♥
1. za	pa	va	ca
2. ze	pe	ve	ke
3. zi	pi	vi	ki
4. zo	po	vo	co
5. zu	pu	vu	cu
6. zip	zap	zig	zag
7. pan	pop	pig	pup
8. van	vet	cat	cob
9. cut	Kim	cub	Ken

nap|kin

pic|nic

Word Challenge

Read across and then down. Be sure to sound both consonants that follow the vowel.

●	■	▲
1. cămp	lămp	dămp
2. dŭmp	pŭmp	lŭmp
3. hŭmp	jŭmp	bŭmp
4. help	yelp	gulp
5. milk	silk	bulk
6. melt	felt	belt
7. sand	hand	land
8. bend	send	mend
9. pond	bond	fond

pump|kin

Word Challenge

Read across and then down.

●	■	▲
1. lĭft	gĭft	sŏft
2. act	fact	tact
3. bent	went	tent
4. rent	Kent	sent
5. hunt	runt	punt

Sight words: the, a

a red lamp

the big tent

Kim's gift

the soft, wet sand

The Long Vowels

Note: The long vowel sounds are the same as their names. We mark a long vowel with a stick.

Aa   *Aa*

ācorn

Ee   *Ee*

ēagle

Ii   *Ii*

īce cream

Oo   *Oo*

ōpen

Uu   *Uu*

ūniform

ī   ō   *ū*   ā   *ē*

ē   *ā*   ī   *ō*   ū

Chart 5   41

Review of Short and Long Vowels

ă*	🍎	ā	🌰
ĕ	🐘	ē	🦅
ĭ		ī	🍦
ŏ	🦤	ō	🪟
ŭ	☂	ū	💂

ĕ	ō	ŭ	ā
ī	ă	ē	ŭ
ŏ	ū	ĕ	ī
ā	ĭ	ō	ĕ

*__Note:__ Short vowels are marked with a smile (˘).

ā   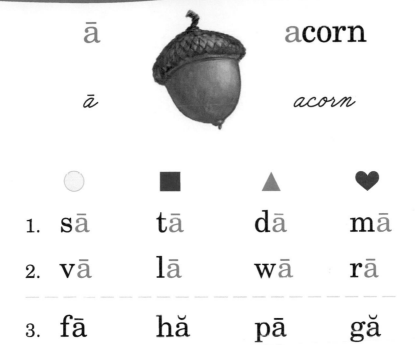   acorn

ā   *acorn*

○	■	▲	♥
1. sā	tā	dā	mā
2. vā	lā	wā	rā
3. fā	hă	pā	gă

Rules:
1. When there is one vowel in a word, it usually says its short sound.
2. When there are two vowels in a word, the first vowel says its long sound, and the second vowel is silent.

căn – cānȼ   măd – mādȼ

Review of Short and Long A*a*

1. Jăn – Jānȩ   păl – pāịl
2. căp – cāpȩ   ăt – ātȩ
3. man – mane Sam – same

○	■	▲	♥
4. gātȩ	mātȩ	lātȩ	ātȩ
5. pāịl	māịl	sāịl	Gāịl
6. laid	maid	paid	wade

Sight word: a

Jane has a big cake.
Mom made it.

Review of Short and Long *Aa*

Say the sounds: ă ā

●	■	▲	♥
1. căt	gāte	păn	quāke
2. Jāne	tăn	Dăd	cāve
3. bad	late	game	sad
4. fake	map	name	rag
5. am	wax	bake	rain

Sight word: the

Dad is at the gate.

Sam has a fun game.

Can Sam wait?

ē      eagle

ē̠   *eagle*

⚪	⬛	🔺	❤️
1. lē	bē	rē	mē
2. fē	dē	quē	sē
3. nē	gē	kē	tē
4. zē	hě	jē	ně
5. wě	vē	kě	gē
6. yē	bě	nē	rě

fěd – fēēd   rěd – rēad

sět – sēat   pět – Pēte

den – Dean   fell – feel

Review of Short and Long *Ee*

	●	■	▲	♥
1.	sēat	mēat	hēat	fēet
2.	fēed	rēad	nēed	wēed
3.	keep	jeep	leap	beep
4.	bĕll	Pēte	dĕn	sēe
5.	meal	beef	red	ten
6.	yell	leg	tea	feel

Sight word: the

Jean has the tape.
Will Pete need it?

Review of
Short and Long *Aa* and *Ee*

Say the sounds: ā   ă   ē   ĕ

1. bāịt   nēạt   cākɇ   bēɇt

2. sēɇk   gāvɇ   pāịn   lēạf

3. make   same   queen   heel

4. deed   date   weak   tape

5. peel   beep   nail   fade

Sight word: a

Sam can see a big cake.

Jane made it.

Sam and Jane will eat it.

sĭx|tēɇn   ĭn|dēɇd

ī      ice cream

ī̆   *ice cream*

		■	▲	♥
1.	mī	rī	yī	sī
2.	tī	lī	bī	hī
3.	fī	nī	gī	kī
4.	dĭ	fī	kĭ	nī
5.	pī	vĭ	wī	gĭ
6.	sĭ	mī	lĭ	vī

bĭt – bītȩ   dĭm – dīmȩ

hid – hide   rip – ripe

kit – kite   fin – fine

Review of Short and Long *Ii*

○	■	▲	♥
1. bīte	dīme	hĭde	kīte
2. ripe	bike	file	hive
3. like	mile	nine	pie
4. bĭb	dīve	dĭd	līne
5. life	nine	zip	tin
6. five	pin	big	Mike

Sight word: a

Mom made a pie.

Take a big bite, Dave.

Review of
Short and Long *Aa*, *Ee*, *Ii*

Say the sounds: ā ē ī ă ĕ ĭ

⬤	⬛	▲	♥
1. bāịt	dēạl	fīne	Jāne
2. heat	kite	late	meal
3. pile	rain	seal	time
4. tāịl	bĕll	vīne	căn
5. fed	wipe	ham	bead

Sight word: the

Ted can see the red kite.
Can Bill see it?

văl|ĕn|tīne

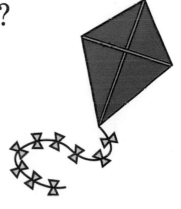

ō      open

ŏ   *open*

○	■	▲	♥
1. fō	dō	gō	sō
2. zō	lō	tō	bō
3. hō	mō	cō	pō
4. rŏ	mō	hŏ	jō
5. nō	wŏ	pō	dŏ
6. sŏ	jō	tŏ	vō

hŏp – hōpe   gŏt – gōat

rob – robe   not – note

Jon – Joan   rod – road

Review of Short and Long *Oo*

○	■	▲	♥
1. quōt¢	vōt¢	rōb¢	hōp¢
2. note	rode	bōne	coke
3. home	joke	mole	pole
4. bŏss	vōt¢	Bŏb	tōad
5. soap	cod	road	dŏll
6. fŏg	Gŏd	mole	boat

Sight words: a, the

Tip had a big bone.

He dug a deep hole.

Can Bob see the bone?

ō|pen

Review of
Short and Long *Aa, Ee, Ii, Oo*

Say the sounds: ă   ā   ĕ   ē   ĭ   ī   ŏ   ō

◯   ■   ▲   ♥

1. wāįt   tēạm   sīdé   rōpé
2. peek   nine   moan   lake
3. kite   Joe   gate   feel

4. tŏp   Dālé   Jĕff   bīké
5. bad   den   line   pole

Sight words: to, the

Jeff will take his pole
to the lake.

Kim will dig in the sand.

The lake is fun!

ū  **uniform**

ū *uniform*

Note: Long *u* can say ū or o͞o.

1. lū   tū   bū   rū

2. mū   fū   dū   gū

3. sū   zŭ   hū   jŭ

4 nŭ   wī   vŭ   yū

cŭb – cūb¢   tŭb – tūb¢

us – use   cut – cute

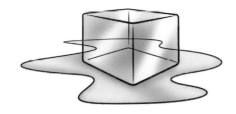

Review of Short and Long *Uu*

	○	■	▲	♥
1.	cūbe	cūte	Jūne	Lūke
2.	mule	rule	tune	dune
3.	rude	mute	tube	Sue
4.	Lūke	cŭp	mūle	fŭn
5.	rub	cute	nut	Sue
6.	use	hug	dug	rude

Sight words: a, the

Luke has a mule.

The mule is cute.

Luke rode the
cute mule.

Review of Vowels

Say the sounds: ū ă ĕ ō ŭ ē ĭ ā

● ■ ▲ ♥

1. gāmé seạl pié hōmé
2. mule wait read five
3. joke dune name jeep

4. dīmé pŏp Jūné căp
5. met hill nose tune
6. lake peel tip hot

Sight word: a

Jill has a pie at home.
Will Dave eat it?

Review of Vowels

●	■	▲	♥	★
1. bā	tē	lī	rō	mū
2. fī	dō	gū	sā	zē
3. lā	tĕ	bī	rŏ	mū
4. fă	dā	gĭ	sō	zŭ

5. ăt – āt¢   bĭt – bīt¢

6. hid – hide   Jan – Jane

7. cat   dog   jet   lid   mutt

8. beef   game   kite   rule   quote

pō|līt¢

tăd|pōl¢

tū|lĭp

tē₳|pŏt

cats   dogs

Note: When *s* is added to the end of a word, it can mean more than one. It can say "s" or "z."

○	■	▲
1. jets	zips	nets
2. rocks	makes	rakes
3. cans	dolls	bugs
4. bends	holes	poles

Sight word: two

Dad has two bikes.

Dick and Dad will ride.

Dick rides well.

Chart 6

ck in duck

e in me

o in go

y in fly

ay in pray

st in stop

pl in plane

fr in frog

tr in train

sh in ship

th in thick

th in this

bl in block

cl in clock

fl in flake

gl in glue

ck  du**ck**

ck in duck

Spelling Hint: The special sound *ck* usually follows a short vowel (ăck, ĕck, ĭck, ŏck, ŭck); *ke* usually follows a long vowel (row 4).

⬤	⬛	▲	♥
1. tŭck	pĕck	Rĭck	nĕck
2. rack	sack	tack	back
3. quick	quack	Dick	duck
4. rāke̸	sāke̸	tāke̸	bāke̸

Rick

Rick is a duck.

A bug is on his back.

"Quack, quack, quack."

Rick will peck at the bug.

Chart 6   61

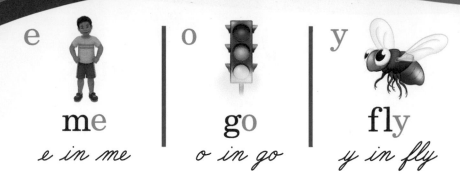

e	o	y
me	**go**	**fly**
e in me	*o in go*	*y in fly*

Note: When *e* or *o* or *y* is the only vowel at the end of a short word, it usually says its long sound. The words *do* and *to* are exceptions to this rule.

	⬤	◼	▲
1.	be	he	we
2.	no	go	so
3.	my	by	fly

Sight word: to

My Dog

My dog is big.

He can help me get my hat.

We like to go fast.

He will lick me.

ay  **pray**

ay in pray

Spelling Hint: This special sound usually comes at the end of a word.

○	■	▲	♥
1. Jay	way	May	hay
2. ray	play	lay	to/day

Sight word: to

May we play in the hay to/day?

We hope Dad will say "Yes."

We like to jump and play in the hay.

Sunday

Chart 6   63

st **STOP** *stop*

st in stop

1. stă   stĕ   stĭ   stŏ   stŭ
2. stā   stē   stī   stō   stū

3. stems   still   stay   stick
4. stones   stove   state   stack
5. rusts   lost   past   toast

Sight word: I

A dog ran past Stan.
"Stop, dog, stop!
I will toss a stick.
Run and get it."

64   Chart 6

pl    plane

pl in plane

1. plŏ   plĕ   plĭ   plă   plŭ
2. plā   plī   plō   plū   plē

3. plane   plate   please   plug
4. plant   play   plump   plod

5. steps   nests   stake   stack

Advanced word: come

Stan plants the seed.

God helps it come up.

God sends sun and rain.

Note: Advanced words contain special sounds that have not yet been taught.

Chart 6   65

fr  **frog**

fr in frog

1. frŏ   frŭ   frĕ   fră   frĭ
2. frū   frī   frā   frō   frē

3. Fred   frog   fry   free
4. froze   freeze   frail   frame

5. socks   plums   best   frost

See Fred the frog.
Fred sits on a log.
Will Fred freeze?
No, he is not
a frail frog.

tr  train

tr in train

1. trĕ tră trĭ trŭ trŏ
2. trū trī trō trē trā

3. trap trims truck try
4. trail track trade trips

5. stack plop free nails

Sight words: to, do

Train Ride

The train makes fast trips.

Trent likes to ride on it.

A dog will try to keep
up with the train.

Can he do it?

Chart 6   67

sh  ship

sh in ship

1. shŭ   shŏ   shă   shĭ   shĕ
2. shē   shī   shā   shū   shō

3. shell   ship   shut   shops
4. shade   shake   shack   sheep
5. trash   hush   fresh   wish

Kay is shy.
Shall she pray?
Can God help Kay?
Yes, God will help.

th

th

thick
th in thick

this
th in this

1. thŏ   thĭ   thĕ   thŭ   thă
2. thē   thā   thō   thī   thū

⚪   ⬛   🔺   ❤️

3. thump   thin   thud   theft
4. path   math   with   fifth
5. thy   then   that   thine

Beth has a moth.

The moth can fly up
   the path.

This is a fast moth.

Chart 6   69

bl  block

bl in block

1. blŏ blă blĕ blĭ blŭ
2. blū blī blā blō blē

3. stĕ plī tră shō thŭ

● ■ ▲ ♥

4. black blush blame blue
5. blend bleat bless blast

6. stone plus thin tried

Sight word: to

The black sheep is shy.

He will stand in the shade
and bleat.

We like to feed him grass.

cl  clock

cl in clock

1. clŭ   clĭ   clŏ   clă   clĕ
2. clō   clū   clā   clē   clī̄
3. clī̄   clă   clō   clē   clŏ

4. clam   claim   cloth   clean
5. club   clip   click   clay
6. clash   clap   cluck   clamp

Sight words: says, to

The clock in the class says nine.

It is time to play with clay.

At ten, it is time to clean up.

Please clean up the clay, Jay.

Chart 6   71

fl

flake

fl in flake

1. flŭ	flă	flĭ	flŏ	flĕ
2. flō	flē	flū	flā	flī̄
3. flĭ	flā	flŏ	flū	flē

●	■	▲	♥
4. flag	flea	fly	flame
5. flop	flute	flakes	float
6. flip	flutes	flash	flap

Sight words: I, says

I can see the flag fly.
The wind makes it flap.
Snap, flap, snap, flap.
The flag says, "This is my land."

gl  glue

gl in glue

1. glŭ glă glĭ glŏ glĕ
2. glō glū glā glē glī
3. glĕ glī glū glă glō

● ■ ▲ ♥

4. glad glass globe Glen
5. glue glide glaze glum

6. ducks trucks plucks clucks

Sight words: to, I

Mom made a big cake.

It has a glaze on it.

Tim likes to eat the glaze,
but I like the cake best.

Chart 6   73

Chart 6 Review

1. gulls   shell   clam   fish
2. duck   black   quacks   fly
3. clean   dust   shine   mops

4. truck   plane   ship   train
5. stop   go   thick   thin
6. click   quick   stick   trick

7. cuts   paste   sheet   glue
8. math   plus   sums   quick
9. stay   play   tray   way

jacket   pocket

Chart 7

br in **br**ide	**tw** in **tw**ins
dr in **dr**um	**spl** in **spl**ash
pr in **pr**ay	**spr** in **spr**ain
gr in **gr**in	**scr** in **scr**eam
sm in **sm**oke	**squ** in **squ**eak
sc in **sc**at	**sn** in **sn**ack
sk in **sk**ate	**sl** in **sl**eep
sp in **sp**ade	**str** in **str**eam
cr in **cr**ab	**sw** in **sw**im

Chart 7   75

br  bride

br in bride

1. brĭ   brō   bră   brē   brŭ
2. brā   brĕ   brū   brŏ   brī

3. Brad   brass   brush   Bret
4. brick   brain   brake   breeze

5. we   flap   glide   that

Sight word: Isaac   **Advanced word:** for

Isaac's Bride

Will God help the man get a bride for Isaac?

Yes, he will see the bride by the well.

dr  drum

dr in drum

1. drā   drĕ   drī   drŏ   drū
2. drō   drŭ   dră   drĭ   drē

3. drip   drive   dry   drop
4. drum   drain   dries   drill
5. drift   drag   dream   drove

6. broke   clips   fry   dress

Mike has a drum.

He likes to play on his drum.

Will Dad like Mike's drum?

Chart 7   77

pr

pray

pr in pray

1.	prō	prĕ	prū	pră	prī
2.	prŭ	prā	prĭ	prē	prŏ

3.	brā	drŭ	brō	drĭ	brē

○	■	▲	♥

4.	prop	prick	print	press
5.	prize	prune	pride	praise

6.	fresh	then	pray	glad

Sight word: do

We will pray.

We will praise God.

We will do His will.

gr    sm

grin   smoke

gr in grin   *sm in smoke*

1. grō   grĭ   grē   grŭ   grā
2. smă   smū   smŏ   smī   smě
3. grī   smā   grě   smŭ   grō

    ⚪   ⬛   🔺   ❤️

4. Greg   grin   green   grass
5. smell   smock   smoke   smile
6. grain   smash   grip   Smith

Advanced word: umbrella

Rain

Rain on the green grass,
Rain on the tree,
Rain on my umbrella,
But not on me!

Chart 7   79

sc    **sk**

scat
sc in scat

skate
sk in skate

1. scā   skĕ   skī̄   scŏ   scū
2. scă   skē   skĭ   scō   scŭ

○	■	▲	♥

3. scat   scuff   scale   scope
4. skill   sky   mask   tusk

5. fly   glass   with   still
6. drape   pride   trail   froze

the big, blue sky
my fast, red skates
a steep trail

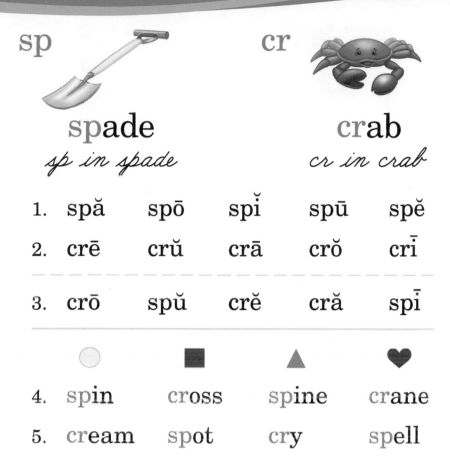

sp

spade

sp in spade

cr

crab

cr in crab

1. spă spō spĭ spū spĕ
2. crē crŭ crā crŏ crī
3. crō spŭ crĕ cră spī

4. spin cross spine crane
5. cream spot cry spell

Sight word: I

My Pet Crab

I like my pet crab.

His home is in the sand.

He likes his home.

He spends his time in the sand.

Chart 7   81

tw  spl

twins
tw in twins

splash
spl in splash

1. twă   splĭ   twī   splŏ   twē

2. spŭ   crō   scă   skĭ   grŏ
3. smī   prĕ   drū   brā   glē

○	■	▲	♥
4. twig	twins	twist	twelve
5. split	splat	splint	splash

6. crib   skit   speak   smile

Sight word: to

Mom has twins, Pam and Pat.
Pam likes to splash in the lake.
Pat stays on shore.
Pam and Pat like the lake!

spr  scr

sprain   scream

spr in sprain   *scr in scream*

1. sprĕ   sprī   scrĭ   scrō   sprā
2. scrē   sprŭ   scră   sprŏ   scrī

○   ■   ▲   ♥

3. spray   sprint   spry   sprain
4. scrape   scrub   screen   scream

5. scrap   smack   truck   grab
6. plume   frock   past   track
7. thy   wish   say   hath
8. flap   glide   drift   brick

Chart 7   83

squ

squeak

squ in squeak

sn

snack

sn in snack

---

1. squă   squē   squĭ   snō   snŭ
2. snŏ   snĭ   snĕ   snī   snā

○	■	▲	♥
3. snip	snag	snug	squeak
4. squish	snack	sneak	squeeze
5. snail	snake	squid	squeal

---

6. scrub	twist	split	crane
7. spell	grass	smell	flea
8. drop	brag	clean	bleed
9. she	stay	pluck	bees

sl    str

sleep
sl in sleep

stream
str in stream

1. slī   strā   slŏ   strō   slŭ
2. snă   squē   sprĭ   scrī   glū

○   ■   ▲   ♥

3. slam   street   slap   strip
4. strap   sleeve   sleep   stroke

5. plus   cloth   flag   slim
6. split   splash   bless   cluck
7. glue   black   slip   no
8. slide   blue   play   flame

Chart 7   85

sw  sw**im**

sw in swim

○	■	▲	♥	★
1. swī	swă	swō	swĕ	swū
2. swŭ	swē	swĭ	swā	swŏ
3. blī	clō	flū	glā	brē
4. drō	prĭ	gră	smŭ	spĕ
5. scō	skā	crŭ	twē	sprī
6. swam	swim	swish	sweep	sweet

Six fish will swim in the swift stream.

Swish, splash, jump!

Chart 7 Review

○	■	▲	♥
1. slip	skip	snip	grip
2. broke	smoke	stroke	croak
3. cream	scream	dream	stream
4. gray	green	blue	black
5. creek	creak	beets	beats
6. smile	cry	sea	sky
7. grill	scrub	grease	grime
8. swim	splash	stroke	speed
9. green	grass	cuts	smell

cricket

planet

pilgrim

selfish

Chart 8

thr in **thr**ee	**ir** in b**ir**d
ar in st**ar**s	**oi** in c**oi**n
ch in **ch**ur**ch**	**oy** in b**oy**
or in m**or**ning	**oo** in b**oo**k
ou in **ou**t	**oo** in t**oo**th
ow in **ow**l	**wor** in **wor**ms
ow in b**ow**l	**igh** in n**igh**t
er in v**er**se	**all** in b**all**
ur in n**ur**se	**alk** in w**alk**

thr  three

thr in three

1. thră   thrē   thrĭ   thrō   thrŭ
2. thrū   thrŏ   thră   thrĕ   thrī

3. thrash   thrill   throat   three
4. thrones   throb   thrift   thrust

Sight words: I, one   **Advanced word:** for

Three, three.

I like three!

Three red kites—

Is one for me?

Three blue trucks—

Please play with me.

Three, three.

I like three!

Chart 8   89

ar

stars

ar in stars

○	■	▲	♥
1. chart	hard	cart	Mark
2. park	start	jar	yard
3. dark	arm	art	cars

the farmyard	Barb's art
my backyard	a glass jar
my smart dog	Mark's barn

Mark can start the car.

It is not hard.

He will drive far.

Will he be home by dark?

Park the car, Mark.

ch  church

ch in church

⬤	⬛	▲	♥
1. check	chill	chop	chin
2. cheat	chain	cheek	cheep
3. much	lunch	Rich	bunch
4. choke	chip	chase	cheese
5. stars	smart	tart	Barb
6. she	go	we	fry

Advanced words: love, Bible

Rich is my best chum.

We like to play chase.

We pray and read the Bible.

We love God.

Chart 8   91

morning

or in morning

1. born	Lord	short	pork
2. fork	corn	torn	horse
3. sport	storms	Ford	thorn
4. short	scorn	stork	forth

Rich's Horse

Rich has a black horse.

Jim rode on him for a short time.

The horse likes to eat corn.

Jim likes Rich's horse.

ou

ow

out
ou in out

owl
ow in owl

Spelling Hint: The special sound *ou* usually comes in the middle of a word. The special sound *ow* usually comes before *n* or *l*, or at the end of a word.

●	■	▲	♥
1. out	shout	scout	sprout
2. ground	mouth	south	proud
3. down	clown	brown	crown
4. how	now	cow	wow
5. ouch	church	charts	three
6. choose	throne	couch	yarn

How did the brown cow get down south?

Chart 8   93

ow  bowl

ow in bowl

○	■	▲	♥
1. low	mow	snow	grow
2. row	blow	crow	glow
3. packs	stump	glass	plate
4. trust	pay	shells	thin
5. bless	clean	float	drip
6. brick	prize	grapes	smash

The snow came down fast.

It fell on the ground and the trees.

Now we can make a snowman.

er  ur

verse
er in verse

nurse
ur in nurse

  ▲ ♥

	●	■	▲	♥
1.	her	serve	term	verse
2.	clerk	stern	nerve	perk
3.	purse	burn	burst	curb
4.	fur	curl	turn	curve
5.	flower	shower		chowder
6.	oyster	power		corner

Kim is on the curb.

She will wait for her turn to get on the bus.

Chart 8   95

ir  bird

ir in bird

●	■	▲	♥
1. birth	third	sir	girl
2. dirt	first	stir	skirt
3. firm	swirl	thirst	shirt

4. burger   border   thunderstorm

5. birthday   Thursday   Saturday

Sight word: are

A nurse helps boys and girls that are hurt.

She asks them not to squirm as she cleans out the dirt.

oi

oy

coin

oi in coin

boy

oy in boy

Spelling Hint: The special sound *oi* usually comes in the middle of a word. The special sound *oy* usually comes at the end of a word.

●	■	▲	♥
1. spoil	boil	soil	oil
2. noise	point	joint	moist
3. join	broil	coin	foil
4. boy	toy	Roy	joy

Sight word: are

Joy and Troy are twins.

Joy and Troy like to play with toys.

The twins will go to the toy shop.

But Joy and Troy will not make noise in the shop.

Chart 8   97

oo  **book**

oo in book

○	■	▲	♥
1. look	cook	took	hook
2. shook	foot	good	stood
3. hood	book	crook	wood

4. cookbook   woodshed

Advanced word: Bible

The Bible is the best book.

It is God's book.

It tells us how to be saved.

It tells us how to make good choices.

I will read God's book.

oo 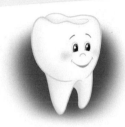 **tooth**

oo in tooth

Note: Common words that are exceptions are *flood, blood, door,* and *floor.*

⬤	⬛	▲	♥
1. food	zoom	shoot	spoons
2. loose	roof	boot	cool
3. soon	boost	goose	pools
4. noon	moon	moo	room
5. brooms	moose	tools	boo

Sight words: said, you

A moose and a goose took a trip.

A hoot owl said to the goose,
"How did you get loose?"

"My moose let me loose,"
said the goose.

Chart 8   99

wor  igh

worms
wor in worms

night
igh in night

○	■	▲	♥
1. worm	work	world	worse
2. right	tight	bright	light
3. sigh	high	might	sight
4. thrill	found	plow	snow
5. hurt	twirl	joy	stood
6. spoon	chops	night	torn

Sight word: do   **Advanced word:** pleases

I like to work hard.

Hard work pleases God.

It makes me feel good
    to do right.

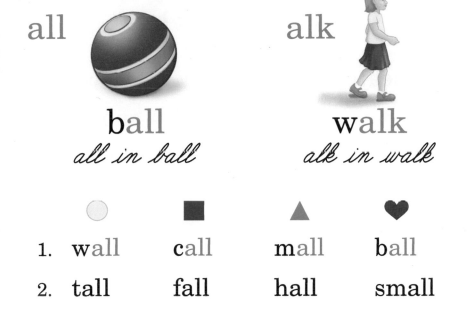

all   ball   *all in ball*

alk   walk   *alk in walk*

1. wall   call   mall   ball
2. tall   fall   hall   small
3. football   baseball   ballpark

4. talk   chalk   stalk   walk
5. cornstalk   sidewalk   beanstalk

Sight word: truth

The Lord is nigh unto all
them that call upon Him,
to all that call upon Him
in truth.

—*Psalm 145:18*

Chart 8   101

Chart 8 Review

1. meatball   walkway   popcorn
2. sidewalk   barnyard   snowplow
3. cornstalk   moonlight   bookmark

	○	■	▲	♥
4.	throat	neck	arm	brain
5.	moo	cow	sheep	wool
6.	mouth	noise	talk	words

7.	boy	girl	hot	cool
8.	ball	throw	drop	play
9.	fur	fir	cheap	cheep

market

artist

chicken

Chart 9

-ing in pointing   onk in honk

kn in knot   unk in trunk

gn in gnat   wa in wash

ang in bang   a in adopt

ing in king   y in baby

ong in long   le in little

ung in strung   -ed in wanted

ank in bank   -cd in looked

ink in wink   -cd in played

Chart 9   103

-ing  **point**ing

-ing in pointing

Reminder: A root word is the original word, or the word that we begin with. A suffix comes at the end of the root word to make a new word.

●	■	▲
1. <u>hand</u>(ing)	<u>pout</u>(ing)	<u>turn</u>(ing)
2. curling	pressing	crashing
3. trying	blowing	storming
4. farming	smashing	tracking
5. clicking	counting	crushing
6. frowns	hints	grows

The snow is falling, Pam!

The wind is blowing hard.

Come out and go sledding with me.

kn

gn

knot
kn in knot

gnat
gn in gnat

	●	■	▲	♥
1.	know	knew	knee	knife
2.	knot	knock	kneel	gnash
3.	south	mouth	shout	down
4.	snow	grow	row	blow
5.	her	purse	girl	skirt
6.	boil	join	noise	toy
7.	book	wood	good	stood
8.	such	chest	spoon	cart
9.	horse	short	world	work
10.	start	sigh	small	arm

Chart 9   105

ang

ong

bang
ang in bang

long
ong in long

ing

ung

king
ing in king

strung
ung in strung

	●	■	▲	♥
1.	hang	rang	sang	gang
2.	bring	wing	ring	thing
3.	long	song	strong	tongs
4.	lung	swung	sung	rung
5.	sang	strong	rung	sting

Sight words: live, have   **Advanced word:** while

I will sing unto the Lord as long as I live:
I will sing praise to my God
while I have my being.
—*Psalm 104:33*

ank ink

bank
ank in bank

wink
ink in wink

onk unk

honk
onk in honk

trunk
unk in trunk

⚪	⬛	🔺	❤️
1. sank	thank	drank	blank
2. think	drink	sink	link
3. dunk	sunk	skunk	honking
4. pink	tank	spunk	ink

Sight words: O, give **Advanced word:** holy

O give thanks unto the Lord; for He is good.

O give thanks unto the Lord;
  call upon His name.

Bless the Lord, O my soul: and all that is
  within me, bless His holy name.
  from Psalms 136, 105, 103

Chart 9 **107**

wa

a

wash
wa in wash

adopt
a in adopt

⚪	⬛	🔺	❤️
1. want	was	wash	wand
2. agree	afraid	adapt	abrupt
3. knack	knob	wasp	spoil
4. honk	stung	spunk	swing
5. sang	bring	strong	blank
6. junk	hard	want	chart

Water has no taste at all;

Water has no smell;

Water's in the waterfall,

In pump, and tap, and well.

John R. Crossland

y  baby

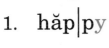

Note: When *y* comes at the end of a long word, it usually says "ē."

○　　　　　■　　　　　▲

1.　hăp|py　　　dăd|dy　　　pĕn|ny
2.　puppy　　　sunny　　　funny
3.　Mommy　　　Jimmy　　　Tammy

Advanced word: when　　**Contraction:** I'm = I am

I like it when I'm thirsty
　　I like it when I'm hot.

I like it when I'm dirty
　　(And even when I'm not).

I like the feel of water
　　Tickling my toes.

But I do not like water
　　When it gets in my nose!

Chart 9　109

le  little

 le in little

Spelling Hint: The special sound *le* usually comes at the end of words with two or more syllables.

○	■	▲
1. mĭd|dle	rĭd|dle	bŏt|tle
2. snuggle	sizzle	juggle
3. puzzle	saddle	pebble
4. nibble	struggle	scribble
5. kettle	paddle	puddle

- Did Jim jiggle the little bottle?
- A mouse will nibble, not gobble!
- Our baby giggles as I shake his rattle.
- Kim will toss pebbles into the puddle.

-ed  **wanted**

-ed in wanted

Note: The suffix *-ed* says "ĕd" after a *t* or a *d*.

○	■	▲
1. <u>need</u>(ed)	<u>land</u>(ed)	<u>wait</u>(ed)
2. melted	pointed	painted
3. shouted	toasted	counted
4. summer	butter	dinner
5. ladder	pepper	winner
6. <u>look</u>(ing)	<u>call</u>(ing)	<u>tell</u>(ing)
7. spelling	falling	cheeping

Sight word: of

All the winners shouted at the end
of the spelling bee.

Chart 9   **111**

-ed  looked

-ed in looked

Note: The suffix *-ed* can say "t."

1.	<u>cook</u>(ed)	<u>talk</u>(ed)	<u>wink</u>(ed)
2.	fished	jumped	walked
3.	packed	bumped	stamped

Note: A vowel at the end of a syllable is usually long.

4.	tā|ble	Bī|ble	tū|lĭp	bē|gan
5.	lady	tiny	music	below
6.	maple	silent	super	pretend

Advanced word: Enoch

Enoch walked with God.

He talked with God.

God took Enoch home to
be with Him.

-ed  played

-ed in played

Note: The suffix *-ed* can say "d."

1. pray(ed)   play(ed)   snow(ed)
2. turned   oiled   joined
3. filled   rained   sailed

4. tĭck|le   t(ur)|tle   sĭm|ple
5. handle   marble   twinkle

Sight words: loved, of, one   **Advanced word:** lion

David loved God, and God loved David.

David prayed to God every day.

David sang songs of praise to God.

One day God helped David kill a lion.

David was just a boy, but he was not afraid.

He had the Lord to help him.

Chart 9 Review

1. anoint   agree   strong   weak

2. sink   wash   hands   arms

3. king   thing   wing   string

4. puppy   tiny   snuggle

5. giggle   wiggle   jiggle

6. called   rang   talked

7. kneeling   prayed   thanked

8. spilled   cleaning   mops

9. burns   yelling   cooled

Chart 10

wh in whale

wh in who

tch in patch

ear in ear

ear in bear

ear in earth

old in gold

mb in lamb

ew in flew

ew in few

-y in rainy

-er in bigger

-est in biggest

-ly in slowly

-en in sharpen

-es in peaches

ild in child

ind in kind

Chart 10   115

wh

wh

whale
wh in whale

who
wh in who

Note: The special sound *wh* says "h" when followed by *o*.

○	■	▲	♥
1. wheel	wheat	while	whisk
2. which	white	why	when

3. who	whose	whoop	whole

4. yellow	rubber	carpet
5. pillow	kitten	handy

Sight word: where

Clouds

White sheep, white sheep,
On a blue hill,
When the wind stops
You all stand still.

When the wind blows
You walk away slow.
White sheep, white sheep,
Where do you go?

Christina Rossetti

tch  ear

patch

tch in patch

ear

ear in ear

Spelling Hint: The special sound *tch* usually follows a short vowel.

○	■	▲	♥
1. catch	scratch	hatch	match
2. watch	switch	ditch	pitch
3. year	near	hear	dear
4. fear	tear	rear	clear
5. chanted	cheated		charted
6. sailed	sealed		soiled
7. hatched	pitched		watched

Mix a pancake,
Stir a pancake,
  Pop it in the pan;

Fry the pancake,
Toss the pancake—
  Catch it if you can.

Christina Rossetti

Chart 10 117

ear

bear

ear in bear

ear

earth

ear in earth

○　　■　　▲　　♥

1.	wear	bear	swear	pear
2.	pearl	early	learn	search
3.	pitch	near	whole	hatch
4.	clear	wheat	watch	fear
5.	pō|ny	tā|ble	Bī|ble	tū|lip
6.	begin	open	tiger	spider

Advanced words: nice, air

I'm Glad

I'm glad the sky is painted blue,

And the earth is painted green,

With such a lot of nice fresh air

All sandwiched in between.

Author Unknown

old    mb

gold
old in gold

lamb
mb in lamb

Note: The special sound *mb* can follow a short or long vowel. The *b* is silent.

1.	scold	told	gold	fold
2.	hold	old	sold	mold

3.	limb	thumb	plumber
4.	climbs	climbed	climbing

5.	lighted	pointed	sorted
6.	folded	shouted	drifted

Advanced word: useful

M was a mill
Which stood on a hill
And turned round and round
With a loud hummy sound.

m
Useful old mill!

Edward Lear

Chart 10   **119**

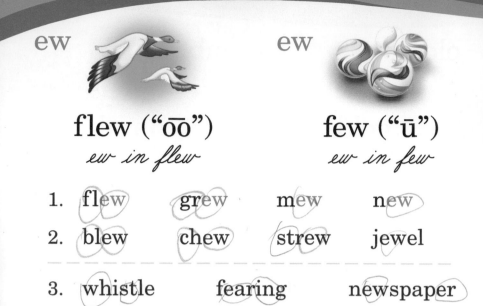

ew   ew

flew ("o͞o")   **few ("ū")**

ew in flew   *ew in few*

1. flew   grew   mew   new
2. blew   chew   strew   jewel
3. whistle   fearing   newspaper

Sight word: give

In six days God made the world and all that is in it.

He made the sun to shine by day.

He made the moon and stars to give light by night.

He made all the beasts that walk on the land.

He made all the birds that fly in the sky and all the fish that swim in the sea.

Each flower and tree is the work of His hands.

Big or small, God made them all.

The American Spelling Book, 1832

-y

rainy
-y in rainy

-er

bigger
-er in bigger

1. sleep(y)   dust(y)   fuzz(y)   health(y)
2. creaky   dirty   sandy   stony

3. fast(er)   slow(er)   help(er)
4. lighter   darker   smaller

Note: When a root word ends with a single consonant and the vowel is short, the consonant is usually doubled before adding a suffix beginning with a vowel.

drum drummer	hot — hotter
win — winner	swim — swimmer

A sleepy, fuzzy kitty

And a healthy, frisky puppy

Had a smaller, colder supper

Than will take to make them happy.

-est

-ly

biggest
-est in biggest

slowly
-ly in slowly

	●	■	▲
1.	quick(est)	tall(est)	long(est)
2.	loudest	fastest	quietest
3.	quick(ly)	slow(ly)	firm(ly)
4.	fairly	heavenly	softly
5.	tightly	brightly	nightly
6.	quick	quicker	quickest
7.	great	greatly	greatest

Slowly, Quickly

Slowly, slowly crawl the ants

Following the leader.

Quickly, quickly run the ants

Here comes the anteater!

-en   -es

sharpen
-en in sharpen

peaches
-es in peaches

⚪   ⬛   🔺

1. <u>dark</u>(en)   <u>quick</u>(en)   <u>fresh</u>(en)
2. dampen   harden   golden

3. <u>dĭsh</u>(es)   <u>crŏss</u>(es)   <u>brănch</u>(es)
4. switches   ditches   lunches
5. houses   teaches   preaches

Rule: When a root word ends with silent *e*, the *e* is usually dropped before adding a suffix beginning with a vowel.

6. broke — broken   loose — loosen
7. take — taken   forsake — forsaken

8. chosen   frozen   forgiven

The lake has frozen over.

Let's quickly get our woolen mittens so we can skate rapidly to Tim's house.

ild  ind

child
ild in child

kind
ind in kind

1. mild   wild   child   wildly

2. find   wind   kind   remind

3. learn   learns   learned

4. stop   stops   stopping

5. hope   hopes   hoped

6. joke   jokes   joking

Advanced words: grandmother, behind

My grandmother is kind.

She reminds me to wash behind
my ears.

I like to hear about her childhood.

Chart 10 Review

1. who   what   when   why
2. limb   chop   axes   scold
3. heard   bear   near   fear

4. ripped   quickly   stitch
5. breezy   blew   combed
6. sandy   stony   rocky

7. lighten   darker   brightest
8. remind   child   kind
9. drummer   loudly   fastest

Chart 11

o in shovel

a in banana

c in city

au in faucet

aw in saw

ea in leaf

ea in thread

ea in steak

ie in brownie

ey in key

ey in obey

ph in phone

ch in chorus

ought in thought

aught in caught

g in giant

dge in fudge

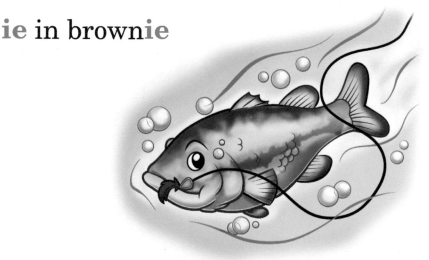

o    a

shovel
o in shovel

banana
a in banana

Note: When *ve* follows a vowel, the vowel sound is sometimes changed: *have, live, give, move.*

○	■	▲	♥
1. love	glove	shove	above
2. mother	brother	lemon	oven
3. wisdom	become	another	cover

4. distance	package	buffalo
5. several	company	thousand

Sight word: said

Jesus said unto him, Thou shalt love the Lord thy God with all thy heart, and with all thy soul, and with all thy mind. This is the first and great commandment.

—*Matthew 22:37, 38*

Chart 11   **127**

c  city

c in city

Note: When *c* is followed by *e, i,* or *y,* it says "s."

●	■	▲	♥
1. cent	grace	rice	nice
2. spice	lace	race	face
3. place	space	Grace	trace
4. fence	prince	glance	chance
5. voice	Joyce	choice	principle
6. circle	circus	pencil	Cinderella
7. cancel	center	rejoice	princess

Spencer and Cindy went to the circus.

A funny clown was riding a bicycle around in circles.

Then Spencer and Cindy had some ice cream.

It cost fifty-five cents.

128   Chart 11

au

aw

faucet

au in faucet

saw

aw in saw

●	■	▲	♥
1. Paul	haul	Saul	fault
2. cause	gauze	faucet	saucer
3. jaw	raw	law	paw
4. lawn	fawn	yawned	thawing
5. rice	nice	spice	twice
6. cent	circle	center	circus

Sight word: many

Paul was a man of God.

At first he was called Saul.

He told many people about Jesus.

He wrote many of the books
    of the New Testament.

Chart 11   129

ea

ea

leaf
ea in leaf

steak
ea in steak

1. beach   reach   peach   neat

2. eastern   easily   measles   peanut

3. break   great   greater   greatly

4. fishes   fishy   fished

5. peaches   reaches   beaches

6. splashed   sorted   sighted

S was a seal

Who lived in the zoo.

He liked to eat fish

And play ball with you.

s

Cute little seal.

ea

thread

ea in thread

head	meadow
ready	feather
bread	heaven

Sight words: broad, where

Whisky Frisky

Whisky Frisky,
Hippity-hop;
Up he goes
To the treetop!

Whirly, twirly,
Round and round;
Down he scampers
To the ground.

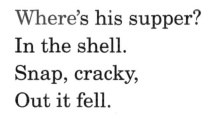

Furly, curly,
What a tail!
Tall as a feather,
Broad as a sail!

Where's his supper?
In the shell.
Snap, cracky,
Out it fell.

Chart 11   131

ie    ey

brownie
ie in brownie

key
ey in key

1. chief	piece	field
2. shield	cookie	believe
3. valley	money	turkey
4. chimney	honeybee	monkey

5. which	year	pearl	scold
6. grew	white	whole	scratch
7. voice	Joyce	ounce	trace

Sight words: says, one

The Turkey

The turkey is a funny bird.

His head goes wobble, wobble.

All he says is just one word,

"Gobble, gobble, gobble!"

ey

ph

obey
ey in obey

phone
ph in phone

1. they   obey   survey
2. telephone   phrase   elephant
3. phonics   orphan   triumph

Sight words: once, there, certain

Eletelephony

Once there was an elephant,
Who tried to use the telephant—
No! No! I mean an elephone
Who tried to use the telephone—
(Dear me! I am not certain quite
That even now I've got it right.)

Howe'er it was, he got his trunk
Entangled in the telephunk;
The more he tried to get it free,
The louder buzzed the telephee—
(I fear I'd better drop the song
Of elephop and telephong!)

Laura E. Richards

Chart 11   133

ch  chorus

ch in chorus

1. chord   stomach   echo
2. Christ   Christian   Christmas
3. school   schooner   schoolhouse

4. pitch   phone   they   told
5. child   dear   great   chew

6. middle   staple   window
7. happen   needle   basket

We celebrate Jesus' birth at Christmas.
He came to save us from our sins.

ought   aught

thought
ought in thought

caught
aught in caught

1. brought fought bought sought
2. taught caught naughty daughter

---

3. buzzes touches clashes
4. costly quietly heavenly
5. darken chosen forgotten
6. creamy healthy frighten

Advanced word: would

The Little Nut Tree
I had a little nut tree.
Nothing would it bear.
But a silver nutmeg
And a golden pear.
The King of Spain's daughter
Came to visit me.
And all was because
Of my little nut tree.

Chart 11   135

g

giant
g in giant

dge

fudge
dge in fudge

Note: When *g* is followed by *e, i,* or *y,* it says "j." In the special sound *dge,* the *d* is silent.

1. huge   cage   germs   age
2. strange   energy   gentle
3. pledge   bridge   edge   badge
4. dodge   hedge   ledge   wedge

Reminder: When *c* is followed by *e, i,* or *y,* it says "s."

5. juice   pencil   fancy
6. prince   office   ice

---

7. jumping   drawing   breaking
8. burner   employer   reporter

Chart 11 Review

1. lawn	field	meadow
2. fence	hinges	gate
3. Mother	treat	fudge
4. lion	jaws	trainer
5. circus	clowns	cannon
6. turkey	elephant	monkey
7. company	visit	pleasant
8. cookie	peanuts	honey
9. school	taught	phonics

Chart 12

a- in asleep

al- in also

be- in because

en- in enjoy

un- in unbutton

wr in wrinkle

ould in could

air in hair

u in push

ough in enough

ou in country

arr in carry

ire in fire

a-

al-

be-

asleep

also

because

a- in asleep *al- in also* *be- in because*

Note: A prefix comes before a root word to change the meaning and make a new word. Some prefixes that we often use are *a-*, *al-*, *be-*, *en-*, and *un-*.

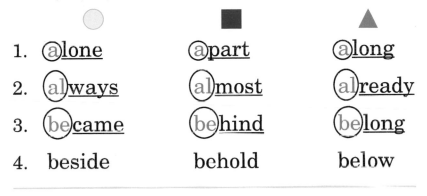

1.	(a)lone	(a)part	(a)long
2.	(al)ways	(al)most	(al)ready
3.	(be)came	(be)hind	(be)long
4.	beside	behold	below

Sight word: any

Behold, I stand at the door, and knock: if any man hear my voice, and open the door, I will come in to him, and will sup with him, and he with me.

—*Revelation 3:20*

Chart 12   139

en-

un-

enjoy
en- in enjoy

unbutton
un- in unbutton

	●	■	▲
1.	(en)large	(en)list	(en)joyment
2.	enchant	enable	entrust
3.	(un)curl	(un)fold	(un)bend
4.	unglue	unhook	unbraid
5.	arose	already	behold
6.	also	befall	aloud

Sight word: only

We are unhappy when we sin.

We can enjoy ourselves only when we do what is right.

140   Chart 12

wr  ould

wrinkle

wr in wrinkle

could

ould in could

Note: In the special spelling *wr*, the *w* is silent.

1.	write	wrong	wrench
2.	wrinkle	wrapper	writing
3.	would	should	could

4.	across	always	below
5.	enclose	unlock	almost

Reminder: When *c* and *g* are followed by *e, i,* or *y,* they say "s" and "j."

6.	race	face	place	space
7.	age	cage	stage	page

Chart 12   141

air hair

air in hair

1. fair   flair   stairs   chairs
2. pair   repair   unfair   fairly
3. airport   aircraft   airfield

4. anchor   saucer   center

5. soon   tight   small   corn
6. south   clown   third   meal

Sight word: were

At the Seaside

When I was down beside the sea

A wooden spade they gave to me

To dig the sandy shore.

My holes were empty like a cup;

In every hole the sea came up

Till it could come no more.

Robert Louis Stevenson

u	ough	ou

push   **enough**   **country**

u in push   *ough in enough*   *ou in country*

1. pull   push   bush   pulley
2. rough   tough   enough
3. touch   Doug   young   cousin
4. double   trouble   nervous

5. rice   echo   graph   Christ
6. taught   badge   bought   cent

Sight word: sure

The world is so full of a number of things,

I'm sure we should all be as happy as kings.

Robert Louis Stevenson

Chart 12   143

arr    ire

carry

arr in carry

fire

ire in fire

1.	parrot	carrot	marry
2.	parrots	carrots	marries
3.	tire	wire	fire
4.	desire	require	fireworks
5.	airliner	another	explore
6.	pulling	tougher	Christopher

Sight words: does, there, two

Harry the parrot loves to eat carrots.

Carrie the sparrow does, too.

If Harry the parrot marries Carrie the sparrow,

Will there be enough carrots for two?

Chart 12 Review

⚪	⬛	🔺
1. push	pushed	pushing
2. aloud	because	enjoy
3. almost	unfold	alike
4. parrot	wren	sparrow
5. trouble	wrench	repair
6. store	bought	chairs
7. wouldn't	couldn't	shouldn't
8. rough	rougher	roughest
9. admire	inquire	purchase

Chart 13

-ful in beauti**ful**	**sion** in mis**sion**ary
are in c**are**	**sion** in televi**sion**
tain in moun**tain**	**eigh** in **eigh**t
ure in p**ure**	**or** in sail**or**
ture in pas**ture**	**ar** in doll**ar**
war in **war**m	**y** in cr**y**stal
tion in na**tion**	**err** in ch**err**y

-ful  beautiful

-ful in beautiful

1. joy(ful)   faith(ful)   use(ful)
2. cupful   handful   playful

Sight words: their, beauty, beautiful

Wonderful Words of Life

Sing them over again to me,

Wonderful words of Life;

Let me more of their beauty see,

Wonderful words of Life.

Words of life and beauty,

Teach me faith and duty:

Beautiful words, wonderful words,

Wonderful words of Life.

P. P. Bliss

Chart 13   147

are  tain

care   **moun**tain

are in care   *tain in mountain*

Note: Common words that are exceptions are *certain* and *curtain*.

1. dare   rare   glare   care
2. scare   spare   square   share
3. careful   beware   compare
4. chieftain   fountain   captain

5. lightest   wishful   package
6. sparrow   couple   writing

Goliath

The giant Goliath dared men to fight.

God's people were scared.

David was certain God would help.

David came down the mountain and fought Goliath.

God helped David win.

ure    ture

pure
ure in pure

pasture
ture in pasture

1.	cure	endure	secure
2.	capture	rapture	fracture
3.	future	lecture	nature

Make a joyful noise unto the Lord,
all ye lands.

Serve the Lord with gladness: come
before His presence with singing.

Know ye that the Lord He is God: it is
He that hath made us, and not we
ourselves; we are His people, and
the sheep of His pasture.

—Psalm 100:1–3

Chart 13   149

war  warm

war in warm

1.	warn	reward	award
2.	warden	warning	wardrobe
3.	culture	secure	endure
4.	careful	careless	carefully
5.	tallest	skillful	several
6.	picture	adventure	furniture
7.	sleepy	sleepier	sleepiest
8.	happy	happier	happily

I love little Kitty.

Her coat is so warm,

And if I don't hurt her,

She'll do me no harm.

tion	sion	sion

nation	missionary	television
tion in nation	*sion in missionary*	*sion in television*

1. vacation   creation   education

2. station   motion   action

3. mission   discussion   admission

4. vision   decision   television

5. stump   please   Fred   tray

6. shift   then   thick   close

7. flame   glare   thread   drain

Sight word: their

Missionaries tell people about Jesus.

Some missionaries stay in their
homeland.

Some travel to other nations.

Chart 13   151

eigh   or   ar

eight   **sailor**   **dollar**

eigh in eight   *or in sailor*   *ar in dollar*

1.	freight	weigh	eighty
2.	doctor	actor	pastor
3.	creator	elevator	conductor
4.	collar	regular	cellar
5.	grammar	circular	particular

We have a pastor
  Who preaches God's Word

So we can learn about
  Jesus, the Lord.

Every day in his office
  He studies and prays

And reads from the Bible
  Of God and His ways.

y

err

crystal
y in crystal

cherry
err in cherry

1. bicycle   tricycle   mystery
2. Egypt   gym   Phyllis
3. berry   merry   strawberry

4. bound   know   nerve   burst
5. firm   toy   foot   cool
6. chant   scorch   worth   slight

7. chalk   knelt   rang   ding
8. strong   swing   clink   spunk
9. smarter   wanted   riddles   lazy

Chart 13   153

Chart 13 Review

1. cherry   lemon   pear   banana
2. leash   collar   house   walked
3. elevator   buttons   motion

4. education   instructor   learning
5. bicycle   airplane   freight train
6. question   permission   teacher

7. moisture   thunder   rainfall
8. neighbor   birthday   eighteen
9. telephone   operator   information

Word Challenge

Watch for silent letters.

1. gu̶ess — gu̶est — gu̶ard
2. h̶our — h̶onor — h̶onest

3. fas̶ten — lis̶ten — sof̶ten
4. wres̶tle — whis̶tle — this̶tle
5. mois̶ten — hus̶tle — bris̶tle
6. cas̶tle — has̶ten — of̶ten

7. cha̶lk — wa̶lk — ta̶lk
8. w̶rite — w̶rist — w̶rinkle

9. figh̶ting — sigh̶ted — tigh̶tly
10. k̶nock — g̶nats — bu̶ild
11. comb̶ — limb̶ — thumb̶
12. shep̶herd — lamb̶ — climb̶

Phonics Charts

Chart 1

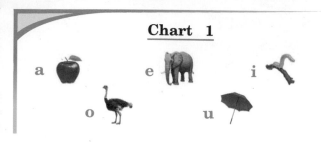

a   e   i
o   u

Chart 2

a	h	o	u
b	i	p	v
c	j	qu	w
d	k	r	x
e	l	s	y
f	m	t	z
g	n		

Chart 3–5

Charts 3–5 contain blends, one-vowel words, long vowels, and two-vowel words.

Chart 6

ck in du**ck**
e in me
o in go
y in fly
ay in pray
st in stop
pl in plane
fr in frog
tr in train
sh in ship
th in thick
th in this
bl in block
cl in clock
fl in flake
gl in glue

Chart 7

br in bride
dr in drum
pr in pray
gr in grin
sm in smoke
sc in scat
sk in skate
sp in spade
cr in crab
tw in twins
spl in splash
spr in sprain
scr in scream
squ in squeak
sn in snack
sl in sleep
str in stream
sw in swim